Feelings

Brave

Sarah Medina

Illustrated by Jo Brooker

Heinemann Library
Chicago, Illinois

Customer Service   888–454–2279
Visit our website at www.heinemannlibrary.com

Photo research by Erica Martin
Designed by Jo Malivoire
Color Reproduction by Dot Gradations Ltd, UK
Printed in China by South China Printing Company Limited

12 11 10 09 08
10 9 8 7 6 5 4 3 2 1

Library of Congress Cataloging-in-Publication Data
Medina, Sarah, 1960-
  Brave / Sarah Medina ; illustrated by Jo Brooker.
      p. cm. -- (Feelings)
  Includes bibliographical references and index.
  ISBN: 978-1-4034-9791-8 (hc) -- ISBN: 978-1-4034-9798-7 (pb.)
  1. Courage--Juvenile literature. I. Brooker, Jo, 1957- II. Title.
  BF575.C8M43 2007
  179'.6--dc22

                        2007010544

Acknowledgments
The author and publisher are grateful to the following for permission to reproduce copyright material: Bananastock p. **22 A, C, D**; Getty Images pp. **18** (Photodisc), **22 B** (Taxi).

Every effort has been made to contact copyright holders of any material reproduced in this book. Any omissions will be rectified in subsequent printings if notice is given to the publisher.

Contents

Some words are shown in bold, **like this**. They are explained in the glossary on page 23.

What Is Bravery?

Bravery is a **feeling**. Feelings are something you feel inside. Everyone has different feelings all the time.

happy

proud

worried

4

Being brave can be hard. Being brave makes you feel proud of yourself.

What Happens When I Am Brave?

When you are brave, you do something even though you feel scared.

When you have been brave, you feel really happy. You may have a warm glow inside!

When Should I Be Brave?

You may need to be brave to do
something that you do not want to do.

You may need to be brave if someone is mean to you. You may need to be brave to stand up for yourself.

Do I Have to Be Brave?

Being brave can help you to
do things that feel scary.

You do not always have to be brave.
Sometimes you might just feel like
crying. That's okay.

How Can I Be Brave?

If you need to do something for the first time, think about how **proud** you will feel when you have done it.

If you feel scared or worried, always tell someone who cares about you. They can help you be brave.

Will I Always Feel Brave?

It is normal for **feelings** to change.
You may not always feel brave, and that
is okay.

If you try being brave sometimes, it will help you be brave at other times, too.

How Can I Tell If Someone Is Being Brave?

When others are trying to be brave, they may be quiet and look a little **nervous**.

They may want to stay close by you.

Can I Help Someone Be Brave?

When others feel scared, you can help them be brave. Tell them that they will be okay.

Let them know that you will help
them, or ask an adult to help them.

Enjoy Being Brave!

Being brave can help you do new things that can be fun!

Try to be brave when you can. But remember, you do not have to be brave all the time.

What Are these Feelings?

A

B

C

D

Which of these people looks brave?
What are the other people feeling?
Look at page 24 to see the answers.

22

Picture Glossary

feeling
something that you
feel inside

nervous
when you are a little scared
about doing something

proud
when you feel good about
something you have said or
done

Index

Answers to the questions on page 22

The person in picture C could be brave. The other people could be caring, angry, or sad.

Note to Parents and Teachers

Reading for information is an important part of a child's literacy development. Learning begins with a question about something. Help children think of themselves as investigators and researchers by encouraging their questions about the world around them. Most chapters in this book begin with a question. Read the question together. Look at the pictures. Talk about what you think the answer might be. Then read the text to find out if your predictions were correct. Think of other questions you could ask about the topic, and discuss where you might find the answers. Assist children in using the picture glossary and the index to practice new vocabulary and research skills.